A House in the Cotswolds

Text & Research by Jane Clifford

Photography by Arabella Campbell~ McNair~Wilson

A Laura Ashley Decoration Book

Introduction

This house in the Cotswolds was bought by the Laura Ashley Company to decorate, furnish and photograph. It does not therefore have quite the same atmosphere as a lived-in home, as it has only been used by members of the Company when working there. However, it does provide a practical exercise in decorating and furnishing a house with antiques, each room featuring a different period or style, and using Laura Ashley wallpapers and materials with a liberal smattering of old textiles in the form of cushions, upholstery and rugs. It will become evident in the course of the book that as much, or as little, 'Laura Ashley' can be used in a room as you want. The fact that nearly all the fabric and wallpaper designs come from old patterns, means that they blend with old lace, needlework and tapestry, unlike many modern designs that demand the 'Total Look' and which can make one drawing room or bedroom look very much like another.

The decor was chosen by Laura Ashley herself, in conjunction with the Company stylist, Sasha de Stroumillo, using the 1983 Collection as well as the Decorator Collection. The antique furniture was all purchased within a time-scale of three months from dealers and auctioneers throughout England, from Yorkshire to Devon.

The aim was to furnish each room in a different style or period around pieces of furniture that the Company already owned. The result was a stylish Regency library, a cottagey Victorian drawing room, an eighteenth-century country oak dining room, two seventeenth-century walnut and oak bedrooms and so on. The breakfast room, which was formerly the servants' hall, and the maids' bedrooms on the top floor, were furnished in pine.

Left: stone built gabled facade in the Cotswold vernacular style, added in 1934. Above: looking across the lawn to the 18th century classical facade of the main house.

History of the House

The house is set in the undulating Cotswold hills, which must surely be some of the most picturesque country in England. Alec Clifton-Taylor in *Patterns of English Building* wrote: 'Nothing is more striking about Cotswold buildings than the visual accord which they achieve with the landscape in which they are placed'. It is true that sometimes one cannot see where stone and earth divide. The buildings make use of a particularly warm-looking oolite that is quarried locally, giving them an intimacy that is lacking in the more northern counties of England. The colour of the oolite ranges from yellow through cream to a rich deep brown. Gloucestershire prospered on the wool trade from the Middle Ages until the advent of cotton in the nineteenth-century and the large number of good-sized period houses testifies to this prosperity. Fortunately for the beauty of the county, the Industrial Revolution passed them by. The nearby mediaeval market town of Tetbury remains totally unspoilt with its pretty streets converging on the seventeenth-century market house which was originally used for weighing wool. Tetbury recently celebrated 1,400 years as a town.

The Laura Ashley house is a typical Cotswold stone house in the seventeenth-century vernacular style and constructed on three floors, with pointed gables, stone-mullioned windows and large, handsome stone tiles on a steeply-pitched roof. The surprise comes when you read the date '1934' on the head of one of the downpipes. Originally it was three seventeenth-century cottages which housed the stud groom and the laundry for the main house nearby. This is an imposing classical house built in 1752. When the daughter of the house married in 1934, the cottages were converted into a suitable home for the young couple and their staff of four. The addition of a gabled facade one room deep along what was the back of the cottages, contains as well as the entrance hall and main staircase, all the services and one good-sized room on each floor. In this manner, it was turned round to face the main house rather than the lane. The Laura Ashley house is not grand like its neighbour, but an eminently comfortable one, with many period features and a more imposing facade than one would normally expect from converted cottages. The outhouses consist of stone-built stables and garages which form a range to the right. Gardens and paddocks surround it on all sides.

Left: the Stables.
Above: stone mullioned window of one of the original 17th century cottages.

The House Room by Room

The Hall

Opposite: View from hall into Victorian Drawing Room.

Entering the heavy oak front door, the visitor finds himself in a small but light entrance hall, whose main feature is its stone-flagged floor, which extends down the corridor to the kitchen and staff area. On the left is a substantial oak staircase leading to the bedroom. Because of its size, the hall has been decorated in a small pattern of oak brown on cream, which just gives the walls a buff textured look, blending with the colour of the stone flags. The landing window which lights the hall has matching curtains edged in oak brown, with crenellated pelmets.

There is only one piece of furniture, a stylish late seventeenth-century Flemish walnut table with a single drawer with brass drop handle. On either side are dummy drawers with similar handles. The table has turned bobbin legs and a flat ogee-shaped stretcher. On top there are a pair of provincial Louis XVI ormolu candlesticks and a nineteenth-century Chinese blue and white porcelain jar with a carved rosewood cover and stand. Above hangs an engraving commemorating the 'Glorious 1st June' of 1794, when Admiral Lord Howe defeated the French fleet in a battle off the West Coast of France. It consists of an allegory of Victory above circular portraits of all the admirals and captains who took part. No less than five artists were responsible for producing its different parts. Prints make a very effective and inexpensive form of decoration, particularly when, as this one, they are in their original frames. Beside it hangs an early nineteenth-century banjo barometer made by B. Condone in a mahogany case with shell and flower inlays of holly and cedar wood. The cast iron Victorian umbrella stand beneath it is entirely functional. Many of these were manufactured at Coalbrookdale near Iron Bridge in Shropshire.

A hall is not a room that you stay in for any length of time; it is rather a means of getting from one part of the house to another. It therefore needs to be decorated with the colour schemes of the rooms leading off it in mind, so that when doors are left open the colours are linked by an understated palette which reappears as an element in all the rooms. Halls have traditionally been decorated and furnished in an austere and formal manner to provide a contrast to the warmth and opulence of the living rooms. The hall, it might be said, is the overture to the rest of the house.

The Library

Passing through the arch formed by the staircase on the left, we enter the library. Like the hall, the library is part of the 1934 addition and the stone-mullioned windows are larger than those in the old part of the house. As they cannot be seen together, this does not affect the look of the building from the outside, but helps to make it lighter inside. The fireplace is very simple with an asymmetrical stone surround, and an iron fireback which has a panel cast in low relief of a cavalier and his lady. Because there is no door dividing it from the hall, the library is decorated in the same colour scheme as the hall. However, a bolder design has been used here as there is not a very large wall area because of the built-in bookcases. The oak leaf and acorn design of the wallpaper derives from a sixteenth-century Italian design, whilst the curtains are of the same design as the hall, which links the two rooms together. To match the colour of the flag stones in the hall, the library has been carpeted in plain stone coloured Wilton.

This room has been furnished somewhat in the Regency style, around a sofa and two mahogany and cane library chairs. The simulated rosewood sofa placed against the wall under one of the windows dates from about 1830. Its most attractive feature is its carved arms. Comparable designs can be seen in Henry Whitaker's *Designs of Cabinet and Upholstery Furniture* in the most Modern Design of 1827 and T. King's *The Modern Style of Cabinet Work Exemplified* of 1829. It is made of beech and then grained to look like rosewood. The reason for this is not hard to find, as a soft wood is much cheaper and easier to carve than the hard, imported rosewood. The sofa is upholstered in an old brown haircord and on it are scattered several antique tapestry and needlework cushions in faded shades of bottle green, scarlet and brown. Similarly covered in contemporary needlework are a pair of footstools and a larger x-shaped stool, all dating from about 1830. On the window-sill behind the sofa is a cast of a head of Aphrodite from the British Museum. Most of the large museums in the world sell very convincing reproductions of some of their best sculptures, which are often inexpensive and highly decorative. On either side is a pair of rather crudely carved small wooden figures, possibly dating from the seventeenth-century which may once have ornamented a staircase.

6

Beside the sofa is the finest piece of furniture in the room. It is a brass inlaid rosewood 'fly' table of about 1815 with a rectangular top, knurled edge on a tripod base with carved paw feet (occasional tables are so-called in the 'estimate books' of Gillow of Lancaster now in Westminster Public Library). There is an elaborate band of brass inlay round the top and more on the platform of the tripod. Brass inlay became fashionable in the second decade of the nineteenth-century in England, replacing coloured wood marquetry such as that found in the barometer in the hall, which is rather old-fashioned for its date.

The method of inlaying brass was similar to that used by A.C. Boulle, cabinet-maker to Louis XIV. Sheets of brass and rosewood or mahogany were clamped together, and then cut out with a fine saw to the desired design. The two parts 'première-partie' and 'contre-partie' then correspond exactly. From it two pieces of furniture could be decorated, one with the design in wood and the ground in brass, the other with the design in brass and the ground in wood. This table is of the former type.

Standing on the table is a fern in a copper preserving pan. Beside it is a small white marble bust of the fourteenth-century Tuscan poet, Petrach, seen here crowned with a chaplet of laurels. He received the laurel crown in recognition of his matchless poetry from the Roman Senate on the Capitol in 1341. Founder of the Library of St. Mark's, Venice, he was one of the principal revivers of classical literature in Italy.

Under the second window is an early-Victorian mahogany knee-hole desk which has had its original leather top replaced by a too new-looking piece of green leather. Placed on it is an old leather blotter, a fine French Empire bronze and gilt bronze inkwell surmounted by a winged female figure, and a black and gold painted address stamp, which echoes the colour of the inkwell.

In the centre of the room is a circular mahogany drum or library table of about 1810, with a splayed leg tripod pedestal. Again the original leather top has sadly been replaced. On it is one of three original volumes of Sir William Hamilton's *Collection of Etruscan, Greek and Roman Antiquities* by D'Hancarville. It is illustrated with beautiful coloured engravings of Greek vases in black, red and Chinese white. Produced c.1766, no distinguished library would have been complete without the set, which was highly influential in the dissemination of Neo-Classical taste. The painted decoration of the vases was copied extensively by Josiah Wedgwood on his pottery, as well as by other manufacturers on silver, furniture, wallpaper and printed felts. Sir William Hamilton, husband of the infamous Emma, so much admired by Nelson, was British envoy to the Court of Naples. Standing beside this volume is a lead library bust of the Greek philosopher Plato. The pair to it, Aristotle, is on the window-sill above the desk. Made by John Cheere of Hyde Park Corner about 1750, they were produced in lead or plaster and patinated to look like bronze. Such busts were sold in sets to ornament the tops of bookcases. Again Wedgwood copied them in black basalt and caneware, taking moulds from the plaster versions. On the wall is a case of stuffed owls, part of a large collection used by the Laura Ashley Company. Nearby hang original engravings after Francis Wheatley and Adam Buck, as well as a pair of glass paintings of the Prince and Princess of Saxe-Coburg.

The character of the room is essentially masculine, which is the tradition with libraries, with its ranks of leather bound books and upright horsehair seat furniture. The placing of the furniture follows very much the pattern used in about 1825, with a circular table in front of the fire and with chairs that could be drawn up to it for reading and writing.

The Drawing Room

Through the doorway in the hall, the visitor
enters the warm and colourful cottage like drawing
room. Part of the original building, it has three small
stone-mullioned windows with leaded panes and an
enormous open fireplace. The ceiling is supported
on darkened oak beams, as in all the other main
rooms in the house.

The drawing room has been decorated and
furnished in the early-Victorian taste, with a blue
and white striped paper on the walls and multicoloured
floral satin cotton for the curtains, sofa and
tablecloth. The vertical stripe helps to add an
illusion of height to this low-ceilinged room.
A similar striped paper appears in a watercolour of
Prince Albert's dressing-room at Altnaguithasach, a
comfortable small house in Scotland which was a
favourite of Queen Victoria and her Consort c.1849.
The predominantly plum coloured floral material

is adapted from a Victorian textile. The curtains, pelmets and tie-backs are edged with a double frill of the same with a pale blue border. Relieving the overall light turquoise Wilton carpet are a pair of Persian rugs which pick out the claret and blue of the curtains.

The bulky Victorian sofa, which could have dominated the room, has the large expanse of its upholstery broken up by a scatter of cushions in antique tapestry, and a rich paisley shawl draped over the back. These cushions are worked in blue, green, magenta and buff wool. Behind the sofa stands a carved rosewood games table, chaste for its date of 1860, its top inlaid with a myriad of coloured marbles, malachite, lapis lazuli, and mother-of-pearl. Placed on it are two treen boxes, a lignum vitae goblet and a cast-iron greyhound, all dating from the mid nineteenth-century.

The circular table with floor-length frilled tablecloth matching the curtains is a cunning device to cover the television and video machine. This compromise does not correspond exactly to Victorian practice: more often they used square tablecloths with deep fringes to protect the surface of good tables, leaving the legs visible. Standing on the top are numerous delightful mid nineteenth-century knick-knacks, including a French gilt bronze dish set with agate roundels, a provincial oak cotton-reel holder, very much a country cousin but whose coarseness cleverly foils the neatness of its neighbours, a bead-embroidered pincushion and a Japanese lacquer box. On the window-sill behind are grouped against the light, a Bohemian ruby flashed decanter, bowl and covered jar all of about 1860.

As a stark contrast, in the other window embrasure is a group of English nineteenth-century black

papier-mâché, with a tip-up tripod table painted with herons and bamboo plants, a work-box and a pair of hand-held fire-screens decorated with flowers and inlaid with mother-of-pearl on a black laquered ground.

The Victorian chairs in the drawing room vary in style and quality considerably, from the plain mahogany armchair by the fire which fits a description by M.N. Wyatt of W. Smee's furniture: 'strong and soundly made but inelegant', to the elaborately carved tall backed chairs upholstered in their original, deep-buttoned ruby plush, with their diminutive scrolling apologies for arms and richly carved cabriole legs. This pair of chairs is a curious mixture stylistically. With their Queen Anne legs and Jacobean backs, they were carefully geared to the antiquarian tastes of the day. Altogether more elegant and restrained is the pair of balloon-backed chairs with cabriole legs which are carved in walnut.

The rest of the Victorian furniture is fairly unexceptional, with two 'what-nots' providing yet more surfaces on which to clutter Victorian objets d'art, and a chiffonier, so called, as it was a cupboard or commode for keeping 'chiffons', odds and ends of material and trinkets.

Amongst the more decorative objects are the baskets of colourful ceramic painted carpet bowls in candy-stripes of sky blue, navy, crimson, lilac and black. The Newhall teapot and cream jug were made in Staffordshire in about 1800 and the designs followed typical silver shapes, with the straight-sided teapot and the helmet-shaped jug. The painted decoration of flower sprigs and pink striped borders is similar to textile designs of the period.

The pictures which have been hung together closely, sometimes two deep and in symmetrical

patterns, include two oil paintings by Norwich School painters of the early nineteenth-century and a delightful gouache of a little girl in a royal blue dress with her dog, in its original gilt lunette-shaped frame. Grouped around them are various small watercolours, prints and needlework pictures, in contemporary frames.

The character of the drawing room is fundamentally feminine and pretty, with the emphasis on comfort. The Victorian era is sometimes called the 'Age of the Upholsterer', and the room reflects this with its comfortably stuffed and upholstered furniture, frilled pelmets and tie-backs. The arrangement of the furniture in the drawing room with the sofa in the centre of the room opposite the fireplace is unusual for this date. The more common form, admittedly in larger rooms, was to place sofas in pairs on either side of the

fireplace against the wall or at right angles to it, with a high table in front to write at. The idea of the low coffee table is a twentieth-century innovation. As a compromise, this room has a large upholstered Victorian x-shaped stool which can be used as a table in front of the sofa, and to one side there is a carved walnut work-table, on castors, which can be moved when desired.

All the surfaces in the drawing room have been crammed with objects, the pictures have been hung close together, and one above the other; small posies of garden flowers and large potted palms add to the atmosphere of cluttered Victorian opulence. However, in spite of this, unmistakable idiosyncracies of the present day have crept in, making it difficult to confuse this room with an original Victorian drawing room. It is simply an adaptation to suit present-day needs.

The Dining Room

The dining room, also in the old part of the house, is next to the drawing room. It has the same number of windows but is darker, as the side window faces North. The small stone fireplace was built in 1934 following a traditional pattern. The most interesting feature of this room is the doorway to the seventeenth-century circular staircase, which leads into the bedrooms on the first and second floors. Such stairways are primitive but ingenious as they take up little space and block out draughts because of their tunnel-like construction.

The dining room has been painted a golden tan, and has striped crimson and yellow curtains, and a brown fitted carpet. The furniture, which is predominantly oak, already belonged to the Ashleys. Two eighteenth-century oak press cupboards, one dated 1735, an earlier oak dresser base and an oak spice cupboard were selected to provide the atmosphere of an early eighteenth-century coutry dining room. The nineteenth-century mahogany table, at night by candlelight or by day with a damask cloth, is not so obviously out of place.

Indeed this room does look its best at night when it is lit entirely by candlelight with two pairs of wall sconces, a Sheffield plate candelabra and candlesticks. The silver plated wall sconces above the fireplace appear to be Charles II, only on closer inspection, the curious curling lines of their brackets betray their late nineteenth-century date. The other pair are Spanish and relatively modern. Immediately below them are a pair of Delft nineteenth-century vases and covers.

Traditionally, dining-rooms had little in the way of upholstery, and the walls were usually painted rather than covered in fabric. Robert Adam alluded to this in his *Works on Architecture* when writing of dining rooms: 'Instead of being hung with tapestry, damask, etc. they are always finished in stucco and adorned with statues and paintings that they may not retain the smell of victuals.'

Dining rooms in eighteenth-century country houses were usually light in colour because of the habit of eating in the afternoon. The use of darker shades appears to relate to the changes in the hours of eating in the nineteenth-century.

The Dining Room by day, laid for lunch.

Above: the Dining Room by candlelight, laid for dinner.
Left: detail of the 17th century oak dresser base.

The Kitchen Quarters

The breakfast room, kitchen, scullery, butler's pantry, still room, staff lavatory and Gentlemen's cloakroom were all added in 1934 and fortunately remain with their original fittings intact. At that time there was a living-in staff of four; a cook/housekeeper, butler and two maids.

The Breakfast Room

This little room, between the dining-room and the kitchen, was the staff dining-room when it was built. It is now used as a breakfast room and small informal dining-room.

Wallpapered in a striped smoke blue and cream paper with a border, it has curtains in a co-ordinating geometric design in satin cotton. The pelmets and tie-backs are piped in plain smoke blue and frilled. In the centre of the room stands a circular table with a floor-length frilled cloth to match the curtains. The furniture is all pine, including a set of chairs which have squab seats in a geometric pattern in blue and sand.

The ornaments on the two narrow window-sills include an old wooden coffee grinder, flat iron on its stand and a brass kettle, all reminders of a previous generation's kitchen equipment.

The Kitchen

The kitchen, with its quarry-tiled floor and large stone-mullioned window, has retained its old cream coloured Aga and white painted glazed cupboards. Unusually, the walls have been papered in a bold crimson, gold and blue design taken from an Italian sixteenth-century textile. The design of the curtain material printed in gold on crimson cotton derives from Italian Baroque velvets and brocades, and is reminiscent of Fortuny's 1920's reinterpretation.

The pine kitchen table and chairs, copper pans, stoneware cider jars, and other old-fashioned equipment make the kitchen look much as it might have done originally. On the walls hang some eighteenth-century needlework samplers which whilst appearing handsome where they are, are in danger of deteriorating in the kitchen atmosphere.

The Butler's Pantry

Next to the kitchen is the white painted butler's pantry, which would have been used to clean and store the silver and glass. The butler's duties included keeping the wines and spirits replenished from the cellar. The old stoneware sink, pine drainer and glazed cupboards remain intact. The simple curtains in a navy and cream geometric design have straight pelmets and tie-backs edged in navy.

The Scullery

Beyond the kitchen is the scullery, which also has its old stoneware sink and pine drainer and a large wooden plate rack. This would have been used for washing up plates and saucepans and as there is no flower room, might also have doubled up for flower arranging. The walls have been papered in a large sand and white figured design, with co-ordinating curtains in a small geomtric design. From the shelf above the seventeenth-century oak chest, hang an assortment of household implements, including a fine pair of brass scales, a carpet-beater and a ladle.

The Still Room

Leading off the scullery is a walk-in pantry or still room, painted white. It is fitted with marble shelves which were vital for storing perishables in the days before refrigerators and are still invaluable today.

These kitchen quarters with all their fittings and equipment provide, in miniature, similar offices to those in any large country house. They remain, because of their size, ideal for today's way of life even without staff. There are no domestic machines fitted into this house, nor indeed is there a 'fitted kitchen' look.

The Main Bedroom

Above: Daniel Marot chair and Charles II oak chest on stand seen through the bed hangings.

First Floor

Immediately over the library and part of the 1934 addition, is the main bedroom of the house. It has a simple stone fireplace, and two large mullioned windows facing East and South, letting in plenty of light. The polished oak floor and dark oak beams give the room an air of pleasant antiquity. Wallpapered in a design of small pink rosebuds on a white ground with a meandering garland border, it has curtains with panels of the border and rosebud design divided by pale blue stripes. The four-poster bed, which was made up from old panelling by the Company's workshop, has curtains of the same material lined with a small pink and white trefoil design. The bedspread, pillows, valance and upholstered chair all match the curtains. The sofa has been covered in a co-ordinating material of larger rosebuds. Scattered on the floor are some printed cotton rugs in the same pinks and greens.

The furniture in this room, which is mostly Caroline walnut and oak, is of a consistently high standard and includes some of the best pieces in the house. Particularly handsome is the Charles II oak chest on stand, which came from the Earl of Clanwilliam's house, Monalto, Co. Antrim. It has four long drawers with fielded panels and its original simple brass ring handles. The stand, with its five baluster legs, has a curved front stretcher. Standing on top of it are a pair of early nineteenth-century painted pewter ginger jars, and on the wall nearby are a pair of Chinese glass pictures of the same date. A late seventeenth-century 'cushion' looking glass with oyster veneer in walnut hangs in the centre of this wall. Flanking the chest is a pair of late seventeenth-century oak single chairs, and elsewhere a carved and painted beechwood chair in the style of Daniel Marot of about 1690. Daniel Marot, who became Minister of Works to William of Orange, was born in Paris in 1660.

Charles II walnut chest of drawers from Avebury Manor.

Charles II oak chest on stand from Monalto, Co. Antrim.

He was a Hugenot, who had entered the service of the Prince of Orange on the Revocation of the Edict of Nantes in 1685. His published designs for furniture and the decoration of rooms affected comtemporary taste in England.

In front of the window is a Queen Anne walnut dressing table with hipped cabriole legs terminating in pad feet, and a simple apron containing a single drawer. Standing on top is a walnut dressing mirror of the same date, a pair of French rococo brass candlesticks, ivory handled brushes, and a silver- topped glass toilet set.
In front of the dressing table is a Charles II oak stool with reel legs covered in crimson velvet.

Beside the bed is another good Charles II chest of drawers, this time veneered in walnut, and which belonged to Lord Southborough of Avebury Manor, Wilts. On top stands a large pair of Chinese late eighteenth-century blue and white porcelain jars and covers. The pictures in the room are mostly needlework samplers, including one by a Miss Sarah Gibbs dated 1841.

In the seventeenth and eighteenth centuries the bed was the most costly single item of furniture in the house. The bed frame was usually relatively roughly made, whilst the greatest expense was in the hangings. To give an example of the proportional cost, Lapierre, a leading upholsterer in the last decade of the seventeenth century, charged the Duke of Devonshire £15 for a 'large wainscot bedstead' and £470 for its hangings.

This light and airy room, with its sprigged wallpaper and matching curtains is one of the most delightful in the house, and has much the atmosphere of a room in a Jane Austen country parsonage.

Queen Anne walnut dressing table.

Detail of wallpaper and border.

The Dressing Room

This small bedroom was one of the original bedrooms in the old cottages. It has a curious shape because of the very deep stepped chimney breast from the large open fireplace in the drawing room below and is lit by two small mullioned windows.

The dressing room is wallpapered in a small geometric design of burgundy on cream, with matching curtains piped in burgundy. The floor is carpeted in a neutral coloured Wilton with printed cotton rugs in the same colours as the paper. The buttoned chair is upholstered in a co-ordinating material of stylised apples, this time using more burgundy than cream.

What little furniture there is space for, is early nineteenth-century Dutch marquetry. The elaborate design of a vase of flowers surrounded by borders of foliage and flowers recurs on both the corner and the pedestal cupboards. The Regency Zograscope standing on the latter is a magnifying device for looking at prints or small type. It has a swing mirror, which in this instance serves as a shaving mirror.

Hanging on the walls are a pencil drawing of *Lady Duncombe* by Henry Edridge (1769-1821), the original artist's proof of a wood engraving of *Danae* by Frederick Sandys (1829-1904), and two pottery plaques. The Pratt-ware *Venus* hangs most appropriately above a Bristol plaque of *A Marriage at Gretna*.

Framed by the curtain on the deep window-sill are a pair of Staffordshire flat backed figures of Prince Albert and Queen Victoria holding a baby, presumably the Princess Royal. Perhaps unusually for a man's dressing room, many of the pictures and ornaments allude to love and domestic bliss, whilst the masculinity of the decoration contrasts with that of the femininity of the main bedroom.

The Sage Bathroom

Part of the old house, the sage bathroom has one small mullioned window with a deep sill, which is the focal point of the room. The traditional white bathroom fittings were installed fifty years ago. The only modifications made recently were to strip the chromium taps in an acid bath to reveal the brass beneath, and to replace the lavatory seat with a mahogany one. The walls have been papered in sage green and cream geometric design and the curtains, in the same colours, are a design of large naturalistic flowers engraved after a nineteenth-century cotton

toile de Jouy. The floor is carpeted in the same oak brown Wilton used on the landing.

Because of the deep window-sill the curtains have been hung right up against the inside of the window and back along the thickness of the wall, leaving the sill free when the curtains are drawn. Standing on it are a Victorian mahogany swing mirror, and a variety of ornaments which, appropriately for a bathroom, all relate to the sea and water. There are real shells and coral contrasting

The Landing

The landing, which is rather dark, has been painted white. The only piece of furniture there is a Swiss polychrome cupboard dated 1800. It is painted in trompe-l'oeil marble panels and has two oval medallions, one of St. Michael and the Devil and the other of a stylised vase of flowers.

with a Victorian Worcester porcelain Nautilus shell vase and an early nineteenth-century Flight and Barr Worcester porcelain mug, transfer-printed in black with a design of shells and seaweed.

The only furniture in the room is a nineteenth-century mahogany canterbury for books and magazines. On the walls hang some watercolour landscapes which although they look attractive should not be hung there as the steam will cause them to become 'foxed' with unsightly rust coloured spots.

Close by the main bedroom is the nursery, which is one of the most interesting rooms in the old part of the house. Conveniently, it has two doors leading to the original spiral staircase, the left-hand one takes you down to the dining room, the right-hand one leads upstairs to a former maid's bedroom. The stairs are lit by one small window in each section, cut out of the solid circular structure. The planked doors are fastened by the original forged-iron latches, and fixed by long hinges. As in all the other rooms in the old part of the house, it has a stone-mullioned window with leaded panes, deep window-sill, oak beams and bare oak boards.

The nursery is wallpapered in a rose pink and moss green design of small convolvuli or Morning Glory and the curtains are of cotton in a narrow pink and white stripe. These with full frilled pelmets and tie-backs are all edged in double frills of the pink and white stripe and the convolvulus design.
The bedcover and buttoned chair are in the pink and green Victorian rosebud fabric which was used as a co-ordinating material in the main bedroom.
The cushions and pillows on the bed are in a variety of rose pink, white and moss green, mixed with antique lace and linen pillow cases. All the paintwork is white, as is the cast-iron and brass Victorian bedstead.
The furniture is also painted white, with the exception of an early nineteenth-century fruitwood child's chair. The nursery character of the room is achieved by the Victorian toys; a wooden hobby-horse on wheels, a doll's house and a perambulator lined with rose pink cotton. The three china dolls are modern copies of Victorian originals. The pictures in the room are inexpensive 'twopence coloured' prints of subjects suitable to a child's bedroom.

This room with its pink frills, iron bedstead and Victorian toys is a set piece of Victorian nursery nostalgia. However, in that era of rigid discipline and spartan conditions for children it is unlikely they would have had quite such pretty furnishings.

The Nursery

The Girl's Bedroom

The girl's bedroom has, in contrast to the nursery, no architectural features. It has been painted white and has cheerful curtains to match the quilted bedspread in the scarlet, mustard yellow and apple green poppy design piped in scarlet and mustard. The furniture has been decorated with hand-painted poppies copied from the material, and makes a virtue out of some otherwise ordinary Edwardian furniture. The focal point of the room is the solid brass Edwardian bedstead above which hang a group of turn-of-the-century prints of children.

One is dressed up as a sailor, another with her dog and discarded doll on the floor, and a third sits, Alice in Wonderland-like, on the arm of a chair.

The Children's Bathroom

The children's bathroom has an old white bathroom suite, with
the taps stripped down to the brass, and a mahogany lavatory seat.
Wallpapered in a small sapphire blue, apple green and white stylised
flower pattern with a larger meandering border, it has curtains of
a co-ordinating striped material edged in plain sapphire.

The Lavender Bedroom

The lavender bedroom forms the north end of the original house. It is a comparatively long, narrow room with only one small window at the far end. With its stained oak boards, it could have been dark, but this has been avoided by the use of a light lavender and sage green striped floral wallpaper. The oak bedstead has been dressed up by the addition of a frilled coronet above it, from which hang draped curtains of satin cotton printed in a design of lavender coloured roses. The tie-backs have been piped in plain lavender cotton and finished with a large flat bow. The quilted bedspread matches the wallpaper. The window curtains, pelmets and bed valance are in lavender satin, edged with a double frill of the same with plain lavender trim.

Mostly oak and walnut furniture of the seventeenth and eighteenth centuries has been chosen. The George I red walnut dressing table with chamfered corners and cabriole legs terminating in pad feet is a little later than the one in the main bedroom, and does not have the shaped apron below the drawer. Standing on it is an eighteenth-century mahogany toilet mirror and in front of it is a seventeenth-century stool with turned walnut legs covered in material to match the curtains. There is an eighteenth-century oak octagonal tripod table beside the bed on which is laid out a nineteenth-century child's pottery tea-set, transfer printed with scenes of children playing. Beyond it in the corner is a Georgian mahogany wash-stand.

All the pictures in the room are embroidered. The pair on either side of the bed is sewn in coloured silks showing baskets of flowers surrounded by garlands. The picture over the chimney piece is unusual. It is inscribed on the back in a cursive hand in brown ink that it was the work of a Mrs. Andrew Moffatt Wellwood, embroidered between 1785 and 1795 in her own hair and black silk. The subject is the deranged Ophelia, after John Hamilton Mortimer, and is in its original black and gold frame. The ornaments beneath it are all pottery, a pair of Pratt-ware moulded tea caddies with caricature figures wearing vastly exaggerated wigs and on either side two nineteenth-century Staffordshire female figures, one dancing, and the other holding a cornucopia, representing Plenty.

Completing the furniture in this room is a handsome group on the adjacent wall of an eighteenth-century Yorkshire low-boy, flanked by a pair of late seventeenth-century carved walnut chairs in the manner of Daniel Marot (see main bedroom). The blind frieze along the top of the low-boy is typical of Yorkshire work. Standing on it are a good pair of French rococo brass candlesticks and a miniature Welsh oak candle holder, in the form of a bureau bookcase. The brass of the candlesticks echoes the brass of the handles and hinges on the oak furniture, which is in turn repeated in the gilt frames of the nineteenth-century carved wooden looking-glass.

This pleasantly light room has the atmosphere of an old country garden pot-pourri, with its lavender, green and white colour scheme. Lavender can be a cold colour, but this shade has enough pink in it not to be, and added to which the white in the background helps to diffuse it.

Left: embroidered picture of 'Ophelia' - John Hamilton Mortimer worked in black silk and human hair 1785-1795. Below: 18th century Yorkshire low-boy, flanked by Daniel Marot style chairs.

Second Floor

Right: circular turret staircase leading from the dining room up to the nursery and thence to the aquamarine bedroom, with doors leading directly into each room.
Below: three lock-up cupboards on the top floor originally used by the maids for their belongings.

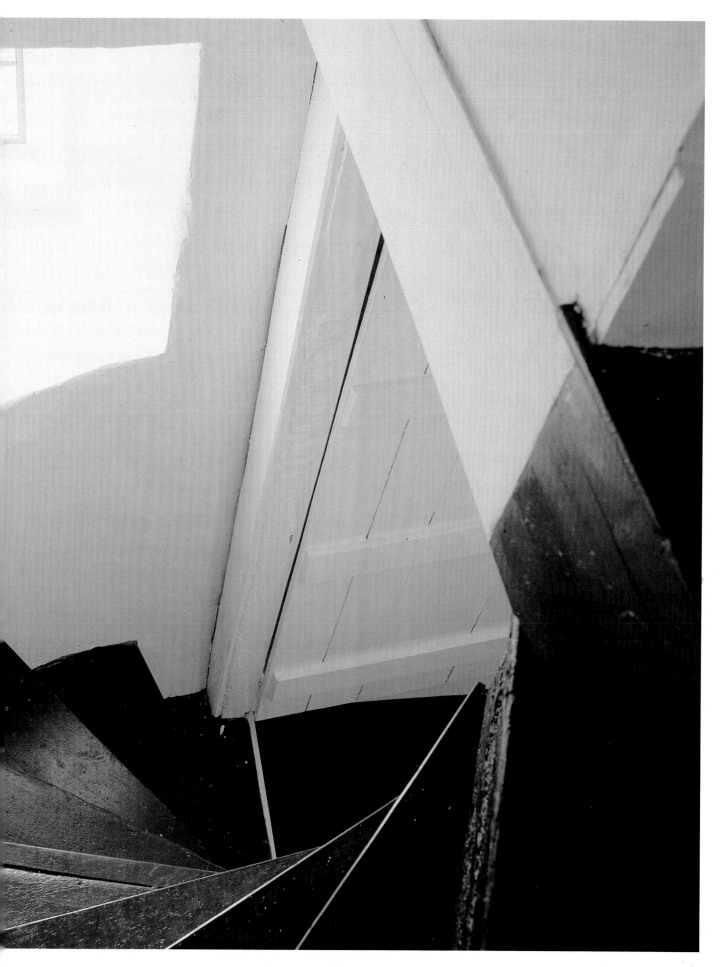

The Aquamarine Bedroom

The four bedrooms on the top floor were for the servants, and the three doors in a row on the top landing provided them with lock-up cupboards for their possessions.

Climbing up the original spiral staircase, you enter the aquamarine bedroom. This is decorated in a striped aquamarine wallpaper, and has an aquamarine chintz of Morning Glory for the curtains and quilted bedspread. The bed valance is of the striped material to match the wallpaper, edged in a frill of the Morning Glory chintz; however the curtains, tie-backs and pelmet are all simple and without frills. All the paintwork is white including the floor boards, which gives this small room a feeling of light and space.

The furniture is all small and delicate. A Regency mahogany dressing-table on turned legs ending in brass castors has standing on it a George III shield-shaped dressing looking-glass, and is flanked by a pretty pair of lyre-backed rosewood bedroom chairs. Hanging on the wall above is a Chinese Chippendale-style fret bracket, on which stand a pair of Wedgwood Queen's Ware plates decorated in transfer printed patterns of shells and seaweed, and painted sea green. When Wedgwood first started using transfer printing, he sent off the unglazed pottery to Saddler and Green of Liverpool, who were specialists in this field. When they were decorated, they were returned to Burslam for firing.

In a letter from Wedgwood to his partner Bentley, in 1776, he wrote: 'I had wrote to Mr Green upon the first sight of the shell patterns that they were coloured too high, and must be kept down - especially the green. Shells and weed may be colour'd as chaste as any subjects whatever, and I hope we shall get into the way of it in time. But this pattern was intended chiefly for abroad and foreigners in general will bear higher colouring and more forcible contrasts than we English'.

Top: 18th century Chelsea Derby candlesticks and other ornaments on the windowsill. Above: Regency mahogany dressing table and lyre-back bedroom chairs.

The simplicity of the decoration in this room, combined with the crispness of the colour scheme, provides a good foil for the delicacy of the furniture and emphasises their intricate profiles.

The Moss Green Trellis Bedroom

At the end of the corridor on the top floor is the moss green trellis bedroom. It is larger than the two maids' bedrooms and has been decorated and furnished in a more sophisticated style, with Georgian mahogany furniture and floral chintz.

The trellis wallpaper provides a light-coloured, simple foil to the dense red and green floral chintz in the curtains, bedcover, bedhead, cushions and bolster. A satin cotton echoing two shades of green in the chintz has been used for an upholstered armchair, the Georgian mahogany dressing stool and two frilled cushions lying on the bed.

Standing on the George III mahogany dressing table is a swing looking-glass of the same date and style and some Staffordshire pottery figures. Nearby is a good, small George III flat-fronted mahogany chest of drawers with its original fire gilt handles. On the wall above, hangs an early nineteenth-century mahogany miniature cabinet, with its scrolled cresting ornamented with fluted brass paterae. Beside the chair in the corner is a Sheraton-style octagonal drum table in cedar. This wood was often used instead of the more expensive imported satinwood which it resembles closely.

The pictures include a circular sanguine stipple engraving by Bartolozzi, after Angelica Kauffman (1741-1807) in its original black and gold frame. The pinky-red of the sanguine ink repeats the colour of the chintz. Other pictures are nineteenth-century coloured fashion plates and needlework samplers, the latter in their original frames.

This bedroom, which may have been the butler's, now provides a pleasant double spare room. The floral chintz and green trellis wallpaper are well suited to a country house bedroom with views over the fields and garden below.

The Memory of
Charles   Hastings
Who De   Pated
This Life   Jan 22
Aged 33   1848

The Pink Attic Bedrooms

The two pink attic bedrooms with pitched roofs and dormer windows were probably intended for the maids as they are intercommunicating. They have been decorated identically with a wallpaper design of pink roses and curtains of a very fine rose pink stripe, edged in a frill to match the walls. The paintwork is white and the floors are left bare, showing the dark oak boards. A few printed cotton rugs in pink, green and white are scattered upon them.

The bed in the first room is a tent bed which has been made with a pine curtain pole attached to the ceiling, over which is draped a long, frilled curtain. One side of the curtain is in a satin cotton to match the wallpaper, whilst the other side, together with the valance, and quilted bedspread are in a broad pink and white striped satin cotton. The frilled pillow case echoes the window curtain material of narrow pink and white stripes. The tablecloth on the circular bedside table matches the outside of the bed drapes and the wallpaper. A co-ordinating rose pink geometric design is introduced on the upholstered buttoned chair.

The inner bedroom has a very pretty white painted Victorian decorative iron bedstead, with unusual scrolled sidepieces at the head and feet. It is infact a patented expanding cot-bed. It has a quilted bedspread in a pink flowered chintz which is then picked up in the upholstery of the buttoned chair.

Both rooms have been furnished in pine, including wash-stands, chests of drawers, looking-glasses, writing-tables and a corner cupboard. The pictures are mostly inexpensive Victorian and Edwardian prints and samplers. The ornaments are Staffordshire pottery and bone china of about 1900. The pair of Spode jugs are particularly appropriate as they repeat the design of pink roses on the wallpaper.

One suspects that these two delightful rooms would certainly not have had so much in the way of pretty furnishings and frills when occupied by the domestics.

Printed in the United Kingdom